Seven Leaves, One Autumn
[Poems]

Authors featured in this book:

- Zohra Saed (Afghanistan)
- Julie Boden (England)
- Clara Janes (Spain)
- Kishwar Naheed (Pakistan)
- Ute Margaret Saine (U.S.A.)
- Savita Singh (India)
- Sukrita (India)

Seven Leaves, One Autumn

Poems

Seven Contemporary Poets

Editors

Sukrita Paul Kumar   Savita Singh

Rajkamal
English

Rajkamal English
(An imprint of Rajkamal Prakashan Group)

Price: ₹ 195
$ 10

First Edition: 2011

Published by Rajkamal Prakashan Pvt. Ltd.
1-B, Netaji Subhash Marg
New Delhi-110 002

Branches: Ashok Rajpath, Near Science College, Patna-800 006
Ist Floor, Darbari Building, Mahatama Gandhi Marg, Allahabad-211 001

Website: www.rajkamalprakashan.com
Email: info@rajkamalprakashan.com

Cover Painting: Yogendra

Printed at B.K. Offset
Naveen Shahadara, Delhi-32

SEVEN LEAVES, ONE AUTUMN
Seven Contemporary Poets
Poems
Editors: Sukrita Paul Kumar & Savita Singh

ISBN: 978-81-267-2110-8

for

every leaf

off the tree

Seven Leaves, One Autumn

Poems by women from different spaces, same times

The coming together of seven women poets from different parts of the world, has happened with a sense of inevitability without any deliberation! Having known each other's works and with an acute awareness of the difference in style, content and perspective, we decided we needed to be together in the same volume. What prompts us to do this? Is it the gender affinity that transcends cultural specificity? Or, is it a shared aesthetics or vision? Our poems, we thought speak to each other effortlessly and put together, they are likely to create a harmonious chorus of varied notes. Transcending political and social divisions and categories, these voices create a domain of their own. The poems selected here inhabit an open space of silences that come alive with a feeling of urgency; while there is a "seeking" through a range of experiences presented, there is also a quiet resistance built into these voices, the resistance to any kind of dominance or exploitation. What is shared is a desire to create new meanings and fresh premises for human existence, particularly for the female gender.

The "seven leaves of one autumn" in this volume are Clara Janes from Spain, Ute Margaret Saine from the USA, Kishwar Naheed from Pakistan, Zohra Said from Afganistan, Julie Boden from Britain and from India, Savita Singh and Sukrita Paul Kumar. The translators of the poems which have been translated from the original languages of the poets have been duly acknowledged. All other poems have been written in the original English. In the end, each poet creates her own world in a language that awaits meaning, wishing to exist in her autonomy and yet reach out to the other.

Sukrita Paul Kumar • Savita Singh

Contents

Sukrita (India)

Zohra Saed

Afghanistan

Lime Trees at Dusk

Jalalabad

My father is a handsome man,
a regular Hindi movie star they call him in Kabul.
But better looking, everyone agrees,
in his karakul hat and rectangular sunglasses.
The city girls chase him,
so shameless these bare-legged girls!
Not even the threat of spraying acid at their bared parts
prevent the latest fashion rage:

the mini skirt.

My father is a handsome man.
Girls sneak into his orchard,
tie love letters tucked in silk scarves to branches,
and scatter chocolates by his doorstep.
He rides his bicycle and notices even the veiled girls

quivering.

My father married a regular Hindi *filmi* girl,
so they say as she passes by swinging her arms
in rhythm to her swishing bellbottoms...
After the sweet-eating ceremony,

under the shade of his lime trees,
she faints from the Jalalabad heat.
He lifts her, a bundle of bright silks and chiffon
and blushes.

This is how Father Tells me to Remember Afghanistan, But I Remember it like this...

i.

Yellow dust and more yellow dust
in family snapshots
courtyards buildings streets people and cars
are muted by the color of the mountains.
Afghanistan is a glittering yellow,
sun-baked into the black of my eyes.

ii.

Pine nuts and dried apricots
served with black tea
perfumed with cardamom seeds.
An insisting hand keeps pouring tea.

iii.

An old aunt reads tea leaves.
A row of overturned cups wait to be read.
Unmarried girls whisper their own premonitions into each other's ears.
A horse or a falcon means a husband is coming.
Is he tall?

iv.

Father says, The Hindu Kush is the trailing skirt of the Himalayas.

At the heart of the mountains are rubies and sapphires with snakes coiled around them, guarding them against thieves, miners and bombs.

v.

A sky bruised from too much sun a rooftop crowded with boys
tugging at strings shimmering with powdered glass.
Kites in primary colors cut the belly of clouds.

Medina, 1979

Mosque is mother too, beneath her arch the dust is Zohra,
age four, eyes darkened with Kohl, named after a star and
existing as one of the ivory columns.

Grandfather leans against the pale blue Honda,
Lifts me to the sky,

Reach!

Reach!

I am his telephone line to God.

Sparrows in a Dish

In between chores, we
sneak stale bread to the rooftop,
Sit with our backs to each other
and scatter pieces of yesterday's bread.

Sister of my spine
We are twin arches on our mother's face
Owned by the moods of her forehead
Torn apart one day… not now… but one day
All because we forgot to escape and sit
Back to back scattering stale bread to birds
While mother looked away.

The sky is criss-crossed with clotheslines.
Smoke from apartment chimneys
Muffle the moon. We
slip out of our mother's constant watch.

In the day, mother lures us to housework. We
carry wet clothes in the cold,
make an army of dough balls,
fold away dried laundry,
wash dishes while standing on chairs
pulled over to the sink
because we are too small to reach.

The sting of our seclusion from the outside
soothed by her stories.

We
give up climbing fences
and scraping knees.

We
give up handball and playgrounds
boiling with children.

This is what growth must feel like,
a butterfly in the throat
a deep ache in the bones.

We
Are two and made for her.
The solace after years of belonging
to her mother. One day,
not this day,
she will leave with you
tucked under her arm.
One day, I will be left
Unsistered (more tragic than unmothered)
And obsessed with looking into mirrors
trying to find your face
in the shadows of mine.

This is what growth must feel like,

a butterfly in the throat
a deep ache in the bones.

Peshawar, Pakistan 1984

Grey beard, pale blue Kameez, full stomach still robust,
face lit despite death, he is stretched out on the floor.

My youngest aunt reads the Quran over his head.
Her face a curl of pain.

In the midst of grief,
Who can bear to snap a photo?

Migration, the scatterings that war creates
Makes us tourists of death.

Dilaram, Heart be Soothed

Tongue
too short
to reach the center
of a jinn's coiled language,

Dilaram

She bears the name
of one who speaks with eyes shut
lips trembling in deep hum. Dilaram
soother of her mother's heart. Dilaram.
Heart be Soothed, daughter with inkwells for eyes
hair the color of dates.

The day she is born
she is thrown out the window and down a well.

> *Another girl, another girl and another girl, all salaaming*
> *twenty more times than they should, spinning my head*
> *with voices that pound, one after the other.*

Can a house not sink with so many girls?

She is tossed into the well
amber frog.

This is where
jinns meet her first, hook
smoke-bodies
into her nostrils
retrieve her from death.

Twice-born daughter:
first from mother
then the stone canal of the well.

Jinns burn miniscule marks on the smooth
skin between her eyes. An hour later,
her great grandmother wraps her inside her skirt and names her
Dilaram,
Heart be Soothed.

What other name could suit an abandoned girl?

Only a name destined to heal itself. Heart be Soothed,
so people look kindly on her. Heart be Soothed,

the heart the girl's own. Her life ever after
is infected with double-sight. She sees
the backward set feet of jinns walk over her back
giving voice to her womb. She will be
the great predictor of love and death,
rain and babies.

Every forty nights, jinns return to nostrils
Remembering her breath, reminding her
of her second birth. Smoke fills her ears
and the animals that she calls by shutting

her eyes and allowing her lips to tremble
in deep hum, flee from the thick
scent of burning flesh.

Dilaram
first of the double-sighted women
twice-daughtered and infected with jinns.

Khyber Pass, 1984

Lost uncle
18 was your talisman
until the Communists came

Only the muted yellows and browns of the 80s
Bear witness.

The Beatles tape in your back pocket
Did not save you.

Red Tent

Red tent of rags,
empty aluminum teapot,
red carpet
dull from dust.

I am seven
in this place between places.

In this place where
Peshawar and Brooklyn
touch
and cringe at each other's touch.

Matted hair
covered in dust.
Round face, large almond-eyes.
The *Wonder Woman* cannister
filled with juice
hangs from my shoulder.

A voice tells me to *give.*
(I am jealous.)
No! I say
(I am first-born and spoiled.)

No! I say
(I do not want to share.)

Even in dream, I shake my head
no!
I do not share!

March 1982
this dream of red tents
never varies or gives me rest.

Haunted,
each time I curl into sleep, this dream of red tents bursts through other dreams of pink glitter and dolls and tea cups.

Each night, the dream proves
over and over my own selfishness.

No recitation of *surahs*,
no children's sleeping remedies, no lullabies,
no scolding cures me of the enormous
No!
I scream out, puncturing my nights with guilt.

How does one articulate a land one hasn't seen?
How does one say at age seven:

Afghanistan has crawled into my skin
and glows as a scorching sun
in my throat.

There is no escape
From this thirst.

Red tent of rags,
empty aluminum teapot,
red carpet
dull from dust.

Tor, Tor, Tor: What use is it blackening perfectly white paper?

Tor
(Pashto)

the utmost black
a black that swallows
the sun blinding
eyes with night

Tor
(Uzbek)

one breath, one movement
stay or wake
the eyes should not flicker
when delivering this command
this co-dependent
one syllable
command

Tor
(English)

Stay as the black of my eyes
where God marked with his pen

the punctuation to begin my soul
sparked also my obsession
with cutting into white hills
needles of utmost black

Tor, Tor, Tor

Stay to toss words
between us like the earth
mindful all the time as we share
breath and commas
nightmares and semicolons
silence and ellipses.

Tor...

Name her *black words*
Rather than *black hair*
Give this little girl
Words like wax
a garden of tangerines
And beehives
For the center of her navel.

The Pregnant Desert

There is a folk cure in Afghanistan among Uzbek women of the North. Every year they go to the desert, Boghaz Qom and bury themselves in the sand up to their neck to cure arthritis, prolonged illness, or a heavy heart.

Three days by foot
A caravan of curved spines
daughters far ahead
tracing the map of their veins.

Returning to their navel,
To the dry womb of the Pregnant Desert

Tinseled umbrellas shield a garden of mothers
As daughters wait
under patterned scarves

The sun crawls into their mothers' parted mouths
Deciding it is tired as well.

The world is a moon while they snore.

Spots in their bones seep into the sand,
unsettling bitter lizards.

Julie Boden

England

Crow Yawns

Crow is yawning out
another ache,
an emptiness so very much
like death,
a sorrow screaming out
a silent pain.
My body is the going out
of breath.

All day I feel the readiness
of flight,
a weave of sighs that
dolphins out the air.
A tidal mourning of a
whale's lament
that echoes out the echo
of despair.

And yet there is no rain,
there is no rain.
The eagle tears will fall one day,
not yet.
Crow treads upon the vellum
of a pain

that our small senses
easily forget.

The mighty worm is turning
once again
and labouring through love
another light.

Crow vomits out the boredom
of a day
and something good is leaving us
tonight.

Wasted Lives

This is not a poem.
A poem would fly off like a kite,
would diamond shine the facets of it glory.

This is not a poem,
not a moment of wonder.
There is no Eureka shouting, no whispering soft Ah - ha.

This is not a poem,
onion layered, showing
slow unveilings of emotion,
the show that never tells, the message with a rhyme - or if
not rhyme a reason. These words do not love themselves,
would prefer to be silent.

* * *

December rained down lines of lamentations
turning streets to rivers, fields to lakes.
Sodden carpets now turned river beds
watched their prized possessions floating outwards.
Some people retired to the safety of their upper rooms,
some escaped by boat,
others gestured hope from roofs of houses.

High on our hill we heard the rain fall too.
The neighbouring field, a patchwork of puddles,
awaited the wellington splashes.
The wood was a forest of tears.
Even when the rain stopped the tears of the old Yew
kept on
falling.
Kaddish
Kaddish
Kaddish.

My hands were two rakes moving leaf mould mountains.
Each leaf, a fallen face. Each twig, a separate story.
Every cone sang the song of its pine.
Rolling back the leaves I saw the gold tooth-silver medal
of their shining; the blood and ribbon red of threads
revealed inside their veins. The browns were the browns
of young boys' shoes cast out on a shoe soul mountain.
And the birds gave up their singing.

There were flood and severe flood warnings.
Windows battened their hatches.
The conservatory roof thought itself into a bullet shield
as the choking drains gargled back their slow death rattling
of dirges.

* * *

All winter I raked through the leaves of pages.
Numbers showed themselves first.
One.
A prime.
One cat, one dog,

one mouth, one voice,
one human life.

Monosyllabic words
manipulated into scrabble games.
Race, bread, smell, sweet, gas,
war, crime, gun, corpse, mass,
state, rogue, rape, steel, sack,
Bush, hawk, fly, oil, rack.

Two.
Two eyes, two hands, two feet.
Two meanings for one number, for one fact.

A hurricane takes 10,000 American lives,
"A great human tragedy"
American bombs kill 10,000 people in Iraq,
"A medium Case scenario"

Am I innumerate?
Do these numbers make sense?

Am I illiterate?
Do these words hold meaning?

Two
Two syllables
Polpot, Stalin, Hitler,
army, rations, air-force, navy,
naming, shaming, playing, killing,
minutes, silence, candles, wasting,
human horror, terror, harvest,
hunger, starving, swollen bellies

maddest
saddest
sadist.

Two was too hard to take in and so I tried a fraction.
1915, one third of the Armenian Nation were murdered.

Next
I tried an image.
If you kept one minute's silence
for each of the victims of Auschwitz and Belsen
you would not be able to speak for another
two years.

Then
a quote.
(Nadezhda, Stalin's wife, before her suicide)
'You torment your own son, you torment me,
you torment the whole Russian people.'
5 million Russians had already died,
many fell later in the purges.

Surely, in the year of my birth, this must have been
a happy place.
1960, 20 million people died in China,
forced into starvation.
It was then that I made a quick retreat
back into the trenches of fractions.
1989, East Timor, one third of the nation
died.

Too much.
It's all too much.

Much safer to go back to syllables.
Let us find sanctuary inside some simple counting.

Three Syllables
history, incident, innocent, Chatilla,
suffering, refugee, remember, invasion,
holocaust, massacre, genocide, mantilla,
Lebanon, Vietnam, terrorist, evasion.
Wasted Lives
Wasted Lives
Wasted Lives

* * *

Naga-Uta
Naga-Uta.
Five for a Pentagon.
Seven for luck.
The rape of Nanking
was a harvest of sorrow.
Yellow butterflies
fly in hope of tomorrow.

Pity the Nation
for their tempests of error
Ukraine's vast Belsen
all the harvests of terror.
Cannibalism
drives men to the shallow grave.
This moleskin notebook
digs words that will never save

the man who stares into oblivion,
whose blank life is counted in syllables
10

* * *

I have lost all will for counting.
I can not feel or taste the waste of lives
except in objects and in signs
and in

silence.

* * *

Hard rain is falling
disguising the sob of the
ancient Yew tree's cry.

* * *

Pity the Nation. Pity the Man
who carries the gun of a grey suited plan.
Harvest of Terror. Harvest of Sorrow.
Playing fields yesterday, killing tomorrow.
The suicide bomb, the hate of Sharon.
The victims of gender and race who have gone
into graves of Anon and Anon and Anon.

We will remember them.

* * *

New spin, Newspeak,
we're sick of News week.
Our Living rooms,
sick of political speak,
are rolling out futons
and laying themselves
down to die.

New age, new rage,
New Labour of love,
of love that is lost.
People who tasted
a real waste of life
are sick of the gang wars
the stone and the knife,
machete and bayonet.
They bravely decry
all the crime as they sigh
'Remember our daughters.
Please put down
please put down
your guns.'

* * *

They're playing with numbers again
and the death toll will slide in the sleight
of a spin doctor's hand.

* * *

Walking back towards the cities
the prophets are leaving their mountains.

We walk, they say, between the dark and the light,
in a veil of unknowing and knowing.
Watch the gnats who dance their dance of corpuscular flight.
Feel the Credo of your inner candle calling.
Set the flame in the window of your eyes.
In this naughty world we need to see your good deeds shining

* * *

Let December rain its lines of lamentations,
the hawk fly from the Bush, the Yew tree cry.
Let living rooms resign themselves to dying.
My eyes will serve as windows for the candles,
my voice will cry out, 'Please put down your guns,'
my heart will beg you stop this waste of lives.

* * *

This is not the time to write a poem.
This is not a time to play with words.

Moth Screams

All night they heard the moth
and, with the moth,
the ticking of the clock,
the planes that flew upon their nightly path,
the scratching in the loft of claws on wood,
the hedgehog's click,
the sudden screams of cat.

None of this had troubled sleep before.
Those piercing screams
had not kept them awake.
The rape cry of the vixen come on heat
was natural,
the screeching owl,
a friend.

But words invoked the furies from the ground
and wind threw up a blast upon the house.
The rain, the driving rain, grew fast and loud
and drove its bullets on the groaning house.
They did not sleep.

All night they lay awake within their beds
where words had flown
on moth wings from her mouth.
The creaking house repeated all the words

that echoed back,
from East, West, North and South.
They did not speak.

The kamikaze moth-words flew all night
around them and the light inside the hall.
Their children found no comfort there that night,
they found no comfort for them there at all.
They could not sleep.

Those moth wings burnt her words upon the night.
She wished each syllable could be unsaid,
but on they fluttered, fluttered into light
and flew around each restless, sleepless head.

None shall sleep now... none shall sleep now...
now none shall sleep, they said.

When, in dawn's light, she rose to change her clothes
she cried to see the damage that was done:
the backless, sexy jumper when they met,
the Aran she had worn as dressing gown,
the neglige in amber tones and jet,
the tiny, white embroidered christening gown,
the black chiffon, the tracksuit for the park;
her life, in clothes, lay ruined in the dark.

Each garment showed the fretting of the moth, where
words had eaten memories.
She did not know that words could fly like moths,
she did not know,
'I did not know,' she said.

Our Fathers

The Toolmakers,
Gods of the Machine Shop,
Masters of the Milling Machine,
Creators of Products and Parts.
Men with precise hands, patient eyes,
eyes that could visualise the outcome of each plan.
Men who spent their lives in sweat and swarf,
who sacrificed their daylight hours beneath fluorescent
suns
to offer us the lives that were not offered them;
to offer us their all
with open
hearts.

If He should come again,
If She should come,
surely there could be no better place of birth
than to be born into the House of the Makers
the Fixers, the Guiders, Providers,
these gods of men,
these Toolmakers.
Our Fathers.

Espresso

Brindley Place Cafe

Espresso *Number One*
(They sit)

Espresso Number Two
(He talks)
Sugar cube unwrapped she watched it slip and slide
jump out into a cup
splash suicidal sweetness up.

Espresso Number Three
These cups, he says, are made for dolls
one's not enough to wet your lips
don't they know some men prefer a mug?
(He exits)

Espresso Number Four
He called a spade a spade.
Her macho man.
No gushy words or gondolas for him.

Espresso Number Five
Was it so little time ago that she had glowed post-coital,
blessed that Eden-Venice for her luck...

before the death his words had brought - this builder of
the Crosby homes that rise from city muck.
He had known the stuff that dreams were laid upon,
while she must learn to call a fuck a fuck.
Mouthing out her pain against an Evesham cup, even now--
she could not say -
the `F' word.

Espresso Number Six
Pulling out the insides of a thing with straps
she felt an invitation: formal, black.
Fingers riding out the dark waves cut along the side of it
she reached to find a lipstick, paint a face to face another
Poppy Ball

In this second city mock Venetian square where folksy
barge turned gondola
she raised an empty cup.
'Ancora ... tin espresso... per favore. '
The waiter, picking up the crumbs that other mouths had
dropped, moved
between the tables
like a crow.

Espresso Number Eight
Somewhere else a figure slipped into a cold canal,
left a life unnoticed.
Save perhaps, the startling of a bird...
a small worm
dropped.

Espresso Number Nine
The woman stirred a spoon to struggle sweetness in

pushed down her feet
raised up her chin
sent a silent order to the crow.

And when the cappuccino came...
revelled in the chocolate and the froth.

Rondeau Redoublé

(Words in italics were found on a London train)

Travelling to London and home again
city commuters are on the attack
packed into carriages , feeling the strain,
stuck in the groove of a regular track.

Leamington Spa-Marleybone and then back
through Banbury, Bicester. Each stop has a name,
but faces are nameless who make up the pack
travelling to London and home again.

Framed in the windows, eyes flicker back pain,
they chew on regret and lament at the lack
in marriage, of children, the house built in Spain.
City commuters are on the attack.

He feels for his brolly, she fingers her mac.
Squeezing on tubes and then smudging through rain
their lives are locked cases crammed onto the rack,
packed into carriages, feeling the strain.

Good girls go to Heaven, bad girls take the train
to gold dig the streets and spend nights on the craic.
Bold words on their tee-shirts repeat their refrain,
stuck in the groove of a regular track.

Bad girls go to London, they're singing Love Shack,
spreading their legs - Mind the Gap - to complain
of tosser and losers, the ones you can't jack
in cos men aren't that bad when you've pickled your brain.
Travelling to L.

Mirror

Moxhull Hall

Here
against the wall
stands a silent witness.
Door of the Past
a cold, clear eye,
unyielding.
Priest of many confessions
receiver of the sly side glance
rehearser of the unrehearsed.
Patiently waiting
at this spot.
Venerated
by so many acts
of private devotion.

For My Brother Peter

Three months after the funeral, an optician said:
'Your pain is due to unshed tears.'
He did not know that at Dad's passing
floodgates opened and the safe, strong shutters
came crashing down.

We are the same tree, you and I.
Born of the same wood,
struck by the one blow.
We are the same tree, you and I.

In the rings of our years
simply read this:
'We are the same tree, you and I.'

Clara Janes

Spain

River to Nothingness

Crematory

The man blazed on the pyre
and in smoke
his sins were traced,
but the god of the fire between his teeth
unfolded a celestial gaze
with no outlines:
I gulp down being
and vomit its leaving
with the beauty of a clean cut,
the sword blade
suddenly bathed in blood.
And you will enter nothingness
crowned with joy from the red
my pious mouth
full of little bells
and my eyes lift up
in a bubble of air
growing lost among the stars.

Translated from the original Spanish by Louis Bourne

Two Worlds

Look at the skin of the leaves,
leaves that are carriers of eyes,
the eyes gazing,
and I know these very ones.
The monkeys leap in the heights
in a dance linking branch and light,
and you are watched by the motion
of the loving tree
searching
to go deep into the sky.
You are the stillness's
smooth surface
where footprints slip
and fall into primordial silence.
Look at yourself, figure of silence,
and swim into its inner space
to the place where nothingness
dissolves.

The Well

What resounds in the depth
of that well
one descends to
down four stone stairways?
The voice of life
that wants to be born
and begins to produce
a soft breath
approaching the bricks.
Love
has many ways;
love is a resonance
remaining suspended
in the air and, crossed
by uniting harmony,
revealing the return
of all colors
and shapes;
arc of light;
a huge wave
expanding, gathering
till it flows into the rhythm
of breath
and initiates the heartbeat…
But where's the water

of this well?
Or is the idea its inhabitant
and the pregnant silence
for centuries
lodged in its dome?

Night

Torches and fires
fringe the verge of night
when the river
is the sky's blackness
and there are no boats on the water
nor animals ashore
and only a voice,
a mantra,
indicates being awake
and astonishment slumbers,
and love hides
beneath the tired skin,
because only that darkness
waits for him,
and there is no retreat
in memory
reviving the days,
and he says to himself:
"Stay aloof, at peace,
for never, never, never
again will you walk on the waters."

Ganges

The boatman rows
and the boat crosses night
toward its limit.
The lights float without fate
on the water.
And the blow of wood
extends,
lending rhythm
to the silence of the horizon.
No one knows if time
is now fiction.
No one knows if abandonment
is now clothing an absence,
a step before
the final separation.
On the other shore,
sterile sand
and a stretch of silent grass.
But the road
appears peaceful
and the oar slowly insists
on the river's surface
beneath which
forms dissolve.
The black sky soothes

bodily life and begs it:
"Lead me from unreal to real."
In the boatman's bottomless eyes,
an agony,
like the love of water.
And the heart opens
to welcome the shadow.
A bell's tolling
falls into the abyss
and spreads in the darkness.

Empty Clouds

On the Sand

Once more I cast the net into the air
and the air amidst the mesh
escaped
and the birds on the sand died
and the sun burned the horizon,
calling for the ashes.
The word without a husk
was empty:
the fiction and its purpose
were left exposed.
Hope and faith, exhausted,
reaped the last sigh of love.
And the birds in the sand died
and, in the sand, the dream grew weak.
Among white clouds,
a sail with no direction
slipped away.

Where the Forms Die

Threshold of snow,
dark noonday,
in the dissolving of sand
someone calls to a fountain.

The wave pulsing
beneath appearances
knows the roads
have worn away.

What movement describes
where the forms die
in that space,
where the echoes
flee?

The harshness
tears
the void from the void:
neither being nor non-being,
a breath
lacking a word... —

Threshold of snow,

dark noonday,
someone calls to a fountain.

And the horizon's just a dot
that disappears.

Roses of Fire

1

I want to drag the moonlight
along the waters of the night,
in them to be silver oar and to plough through
and to be one with star
that awakens the sleeping path of light.

And then to lose myself
in a far-off enveloping halo,
to be fixed in love by unattainable,
without being noticed,
and thus to remain
in the desoblivion of the day.

2

The wind has licked
leaves of rain
and the storm
with lashes of lightning
alerts the shadows.
The sweet feline approaches.
With a stubborn rhythm
pure fusion illuminates
its gentle touch.

Violent contours surrender
to the vivid beating
that joins us to the cosmos.
And stormy winds
and perfumes
envelop the watchful soul.

3

Star of twilight between the trees,
voyage to the distant days of infancy
: the mountain's back
was a cloak of dreams.
Each trunk, the beloved's body,
the immutable waters
traced the ecstasy
and in the reddish line of twilight
branches rubbed against each other
setting fire to the heart.
Star of sunset, path
towards landscapes even more remote,
with my eyes I can attain you
and before the shadow overtakes me
I withdraw into myself
and go back to the days of Utnapistim
and contemplate the lands
bathed by the Euphrates.

4

Waterfalls of aroma
of lindens in bloom
hasten the whiteness:
black tyrannizes the space.

Enveloped in flames,
a violet sphere
falls dizzy.
The gentle water
takes refuge in extended waves.
The crater of night
reveals the point of nothingness.

It is a gift of clarity
to recognize the signs.

5

Bonfire is the sun
at the moment
when it defeats the day.
The heart surrenders,
and among the ribbons of smoke
of graying ash
spread by the birds,
the longing for ascent
flutters in pursuit of
oncoming night,
shadow of love,
that alone makes way for
the vision of light.

6

Night
with its sieve of shadow
sifts only stars.
In my fainting they fall
crossing the black veil

that like a shroud covers me.
The meek sleep
welcomes its clarity,
that silver thread
that is lost
and then found
with the dawn.

7

At the onset of moonlight
plants and trees
collect themselves;
and in the halo that reveals our center
the gaze is transfixed.
White branches of harmony
fill the nocturnal hour.
The silent orb
readies its heart for dawn.

8

Before the light breaks in
and its restless dialogue with the shadows
can inhabit the valleys of repose,
I enclose mist and silence
and enclose myself within so
that love can grow,
I make way only for the birds' song.

Translated from the original Spanish by Anne Pasero

Kishwar Naheed

Pakistan

Accusation of a Dream for Being Alive

I was made to be born to cry on my own grave.
That suicide does not make you contented.
I have given birth, but to whom?
Its fragments have neither a monument
nor remnants nor dust.
I promise to meet with life.
I went to see life, but on my way
the island of helplessness was there.
I diverted my path and went to see death.
Death was wearing the mask of tears.
She gave anorexia to my pen.
And then my hands refused to write
the words of love and life.
Who can count the drops coming
in the rows of rain from sky to earth?
Likewise I cannot count the moments
I have spent trying to catch the thief,
And the thief was the wound of my heart,
my hands were the thief,
hands that go up to my neck
but don't end the story.
The hands that take me to
the island of helplessness,
Promise to come back and
never come back.

Translated from the original Urdu by Kishwar Naheed, edited and adapted by Naomi Shihab Nye

We Sinful Women

It is we sinful women
who are not awed by the grandeur of those who wear
gowns
who don't sell our lives
who don't bow our heads
who don't fold our hands together

It is we sinful women
while those who sell the harvests of our bodies
become exalted
become distinguished
become the just princes of the material world.

It is we sinful women
who come out raising the banner of truth
against barricades of lies on the highways
who find stories of persecution piled on each threshold
who find the tongues which could speak have been
severed.

It is we sinful women.
Now, even if the night gives chase
these eyes shall not be put out.
For the wall which has been razed
don't insist now on raising it again.

It is we sinful women
who are not awed by the grandeur of those who wear
gowns
who don't sell our bodies
who don't bow our heads
who don't fold our hands together.

Translated from the original Urdu by Rukhsana Ahmad

Kishwar Naheed

All bonds
All thirty-eight years of life
Have ripened into your cheeks and hair
Like the glowing forms of life.
All bonds
Break in the crush of spent passions
And waning seasons
Like falling unripe fruit.

Kishwar Naheed,
An oyster with sealed lips,
Woman of the past,
Woman of today,
Afflicted,
You speak from the shore
To the winds of life's ocean
To move the feet of mountain.

Kishwar Naheed,
No one speaks here.
No one wants to know
The words of speaking glances.

The fish slipping from the hand
Turns fear into hate.

Kishwar Naheed,
The desire to see you silent
Billows up even from the grave.
But speech is urgent
When listening is a crime.
Now I can see
Expressions which daunted me
Strike fear everywhere.

Translated from the original Urdu by Baidar Bakht and Derek M. Cohen

How Crazy are Those who Love you So Much

With words of chastity he adorned my hands,
chained my feet like prisoners,
and called it modesty.
How sweet and pleasant it sounds,
like a diamond,
like the gleam of a knife!
He says: 'What more can you ask for?
Walls of marble, clean and shining
to keep you safe. The gold lock and chain
on big, solid black mahogany doors
at least show that it's all for you,
for your security, for your love.'

How lovingly and hopefully built,
this home full of ideals and dreams!
It's been tested with screams,
making sure that if a sound
dare penetrate some crevice
it will turn to foam, exhausted,
and nothing will get through.

'Tenderly, for you, for your love
this home, this throne, these marble walls.
All for you, my dear,
all because I love you!'

Translated from the original Urdu by Mahmood Jamal

Nightmare

The goat awaits slaughter
and I wait for the morning
for every morning I am slaughtered at my desk
for telling lies.
This is my price.

Like fresh graves,
faces smoothly caked with powder
come to meet me
In the graveyard of minds only such adornments seem
appropriate.

I and my country were born together
but we both lost our vision in our childhood.
I have not seen bread.
In my imagination I picture it and eat it.
Many of my generation dream only of bread.

In my country women look at the crescent moon and
pray
And shelve all the rest of their prayers for the first day of
the next
moon.

Even after they have stamped permits for a second marriage
with
their own thumbs

they pray when they see the first moon of the month.
Perhaps to attain a better afterlife for liars like us.

We sing praises of our warlike courage
flies assault us.
A sword taller than ourselves we claim as
our inheritance
Decorating our tongues with our ancestral colours.

Those who live in rusty times amongst rusty tongues
are petty officials.

'The one who's "out" had everything wrong
the one who's "in" has everything right,'
only rusty tongues would say that.
Now even the ironmonger, who makes the sword,
assumes
it is he who writes victory.

Translated from the original Urdu by Rukhsana Ahmad

Anticlockwise

Even if my eyes become the soles of your feet
even so, the fear will not leave you that though I cannot see
I can feel bodies and sentences
like a fragrance.
Even if, for my own safety,
I rub my nose in the dirt till it becomes invisible
even so, this fear will not leave you
that though I cannot smell
I can still say something.
Even if my lips, singing praises of your godliness
become dry and soulless even so, this fear will not leave you
that though I cannot speak
I can still walk.
Even after you have tied the chains of domesticity,
shame and modesty around my feet
even after you have paralysed me
this fear will not leave you
that even though I cannot walk
I can still think.
Your fear
of my being free, being alive
and able to think
might lead you, who knows, into what travails.

Translated from the original Urdu by Rukhsana Ahmad

Dream Colours

I had thought
That I would change dreams like clothes
And be fresh each time.

I took out dreams from the old box
But they had the stale smell
of things kept for a very long time
And the dreams were moist.

I put them in the sun
To dry, freshen them up.

The colours of each dream had faded
At the folds
They could be recognized from their appearance.
The colour of dreams of love
Had turned from pomegranate red
To dull liver-colour

The colour of dreams of togetherness
From sky-blue was a dirty shade of milk.

The colour of dreams of promises
From fiery-red

Had burned down to cinders,
the colour of burnt embers.

The colour of dreams of mother's love
From leafy-green
Was a wrinkled yellow.

I put dreams of every colour in the sun.
The touch of heat turned dreams into questions
My smile, my eyes, everything I say or do
Became a question.

I turned to books to get an answer
But with one touch of my hand
The books came crashing down.

Ants were scurrying past
I too joined their file
But they gave me no importance
And continued their journey.

With my questions I came and stood in the window
In front of me was a court

Every day the court is in session and every day a judgment
I turned over my assets to the court

I was condemned for the crime of possessing
Contraband dreams and illegal questions
And given fourteen years in prison

Before going to the jail
I came home to collect my clothes

And I saw
There was not a single dream in the sun

Only a few cockroaches
Struggling
Upside down.

Translated from the original Urdu by Asif Farrukhi

Tell the Gods

The day death comes for me
Let it rain
As if the downpour does not know how to stop
And people forget how to mark the difference
Between tears and rain.

The day death comes for me
Let there be so many flowers
That eyes may not stop and stare
At anything else,
Flames leave their wicker in the lamp
To go with me,
Talking,
Smiling.

The day death comes for me
Let all baby birds in their nests
Grow wings
All whispers turn to music
And all sobs into a golden warbling.

The day death comes for me
Let it come
accepting this one condition of mine,
That it should first come to me alive

Play with me in the courtyard,
Learn what it means to be alive
And then do what it will.

The day death comes for me
Let the sun forget to set
And let not light be buried with me.

Translated from the original Urdu by Asif Farrukhi

A Snapshot of Ramallah

Nothing is left in the room
A part of the wall
and a shell of the window
Are all that remain.
A daily potato for food
And as far as the eyes can see,
Dead bodies without coffins
And Israeli tanks roaming around.
Even the breeze
Comes soaked in the smell of blood.
The suicide bombers
Must be boys and girls of fifteen or sixteen,
But their love for the land
Must be at least fifty years old.
They were in quest of their land
To live their lives
and even to die.
They became everlasting in their search
But there is nothing left in the room.

Translated from the original Urdu by Asif Farrukhi

Commonplace Miracles

I heard somebody calling out with love,
I followed that call
I keep walking and the earth does not come to an end.
The calling voices
Are sometimes in front of me And sometimes behind.

Harvests ripening in the fields
Narrated accounts of journeys still to come.
I stopped by the potter
I thought I will give shape to the face,
I will form the figure
At whose beck and call
The earth could not come to an end.
But pouring rain did not let me complete the features.
Parted lips kept opening and asking me
How does one mend dreams
How does one cross rivers made out of storms
My feet were tired before reaching the threshold of answers
I go down on my knees and begin to move,
I keep the wick of the lamp on the palm of my hand,
I read the thirst of birds in their nests,
The earth comes to an end
But not my journey.

Translated from the original Urdu by Asif Farrukhi

Let's Talk About It

We will be together for dinner today
With the solemn promise
That neither will you bring along any slander
Nor I bring forth the taste of any thirst of mine

Like two new persons getting to know each other
We will sit at the same table
And look at the receding sea
Without thinking of it as a mirror to our insults.
We will not let the regrets brimming our eyes
Be decorated
With the smudge of tears on our faces.
We will not add the sum of our sorrows
To the cheque for the meal.
After all these decisions
Why do we need another decision?
Let us go to the moon.
It will be fun to talk about this over dinner.

Translated from the original Urdu by Asif Farrukhi

Mankind on Trial

Somebody asked the judge,
What is punishment?
He replied, "Life."

Somebody asked a handcuffed old woman
What is imprisonment?
She replied, "Obeying Orders."
Somebody asked the jailer
Locked away inside his jail,
What is the prison cell?
He replied, "The darkness in you."
Who were the people asking such questions?
Countless people
But only one woman standing up to respond,
Tahira Abdullah.
In view of all such questions,
Tahira pronounced the verdict
'The present order should be placed
Under immediate arrest
And mankind should be free
From all sentences'.

Translated from the original Urdu by Asif Farrukhi

The Poison Cup of Mother's Love

You look at me and become sad
a sadness which reeks of boredom
You meet me and make an effort to come back
an effort which hints of symbols of fading attractions
You sit next to me and are in doubt
A doubt with the overpowering desire to move away.
Walking along with me you do not feel any pleasantness
This too is like carrying a heavy burden
The burden of continuing a relationship
The burden of having to say something,
The burden of insisting on some kind of love!
Thank you for carrying such burdens
And for letting it be known to me
that you paid its price from overseas
Why did I not insist to you
That carrying your burden for nine months,
I never let a mother's love become a burden for you.
First I became a shack-laborer.
Now earning the wages of emotions,
I have turned into a tornado,
A whirlwind in the desert of love,
People look at it and make-up stories.

Translated from the original Urdu by Asif Farrukhi

Ute Margaret Saine

U.S.A.

Dream Boat

You are the ship I ride seaside
I've clambered on board of you
to end the rip of a dire sea of roiling troubles
in your extended rolling bliss
I sleep dream-wrapped in our love

I cherish your smile as a child's
embrace your moods like wind
I kiss your crackling summer brow
as we sway and rock in the breeze
and weave my redirected limbs around
your ever-shifting wooden core

You are the ship I ride astride
we sail together over the syrts
we've crossed the Sargasso Sea
the troubled troubling waters
and also windless horse latitudes

And now we have only left to go
the other Seven Seas

Afternoon

The sun puts the clouds
on the table
between the wine glasses
and the olives
a piece of luminous sky
between floating smiles
a bit of today's heaven
that's come down to us
right here looking into
each other's eyes

Child's Play

JJeux d'enfant by Georges Bizet

After Trumpet and Drum
comes The Doll
then The Top

After Rocking Horse
and Soap Bubbles
comes the second last game
mari et femme:

Husband and Wife
something truly
child's play

A Handful of Haiku

the wind's wings closing
over my heart stir me like
music from your heart

passing with delight
into this obscurity:
each other's embrace

a water caress
that presses and sucks on me
just like a lover

an afternoon swoon
you inhabit my body
seagulls cry for us

nights of a woman
let the corpse lie in its best
state of splendid bliss

Crystal Cove, California

la danza curva del agua en la orilla
the curvy dance of water on the shore
Lorca

Sand patient
to the impatient
imprint of water
rivulets etching
light and dark panes
aureoles branch off
stretch to leafy designs

Sand that the water ferries
grain for grain out to sea
and water carries it back
settling concentric
dripping sliding hillocks
surround restless rivulet springs

Sand slipping through placid
puddles left by the surge
of the last tide

Sand a tacit placid river
overwhelmed by itself
swept to and fro by the tide

the pull of earth and water
tugging at each other
pushing and pulling
fusing to consummate

Two entwined lovers
consumed

My Home Is Words

If I didn't have my home in my heart and brain
I would call myself homeless.

–Goran Simiæ

My home is not language not even
Mutter Sprache Sprache als Heimat
mother tongue language as homeland
language sounds far too grand
or it may sound too narrow
one language and lots of mistakes

My home out here is under a palm
or an apple tree somewhere else
I may have been born not knowing
in a white or a red cabbage field

My home is made just of words
far-flung fluttering tatters of words
words stacked like shredded newsprint
that shuffle and creak like cardboard

My home wafts in the breeze
and fans the inner dinner flames
my home is on the move I move it
as it moves me as a snail its shell

My home is made of homemade words
that form out of homespun chores
sail along alone sans bridge or boat
stream from language to language

What may be your bun is my pun
even involuntary I oscillate
luxuriate in murky transparence
or butterfly wings shining colors

My home is made of these words
and more to come I want to invent
new words in any tongue
words on my tongue
and then give you some

Cutting Away Words

I the sculptress
Cut away the words
Not necessary
The bulk of a body
Unwelcome
Or disturbing.

I the sculptress
wishing to be called
the unerring beholder
of world and body
body and word

Before I slip up again
Cutting a gouge and a gash
Into my confidence

Door

for R.F.

Door
we pass through
or stop at the threshold
door
we take the inside out
with us when we go
through the flying wings of the
door
we bring the outside in
when we come back
door
I furtively look out
impatient for your return
door
that sees me time after time
crying and rejoicing
door
waiting between the past and the now
door
at which to seize your image
that lifts my body
to its climax
door

into another world
your world through the
door
that we close behind us
to be in the room
to be in the space
of each other
the air of our breaths
door
doorless windowless with the
doors
and windows of our bodies
wide open to the clouds

The 'In the Dream Gardens' Haikus

love, word on my lips
had fallen asleep crying
you kissed it awake

be there like the sky
like one earth and many stars
and let me move you

open sea, open
your eyes, wide windows, wide doors
till we float on light

requiebros quiebran
mis sentidos abiertos
tiemblan al verte

awake in the night
we swim with starfish and stars
toward the morning light

eyes tear, voices sigh
as we swim and sail in a
sea of each other

lights in the waters
clouds drifting under bridges
inside me your eyes

in the dream gardens
by wind, sun, clouds and the sea
they found us kissing

The 'We' Haikus

we are like nothing
I have ever known, you've come
to me like a dream

we call our hunger
we call up this immense thirst
to quench each other

we toss together
your madness and my madness
the fun house of smiles

we pass our desires
like a contagious disease
with shivers and sighs

we are a small skiff
floating on waters of desire
hold on to your hat

we run through the springs
play in the fountains of love
wet, wet and laughing

we make things happen
we mirror lights and light stars
in stellar lagoons

we kiss, our words slide
directly from tongue to tongue
glide straight to our hearts

The 'You and I' Haikus

your star is alive
blinking on my horizon
I stretch and crave it

I lose my balance
I hold on to your body
embracing we dance

your hands are like roots
of roses, reach deep inside
the earth my body

I feel like the earth
your hands caress the body
till it heaves with life

you are like nothing
I have ever known, you've come
to me like a dream

Lilies

Lilies, exuberant curves of sexless
angel guests on this earth, velvet petals
worn threadbare to a shine.

Veterans' Day

Another Veterans' Day, perhaps
the promise serenely to end wars,
but not the tranquil kisses between us.

Circe

She has changed them from men
into animals to serve her
she locks them in a corral
for further use and purpose

She hands them dishes with salt
and water, they lap and slurp it up
and then lick and lick her hand
she waits and waits, then she goes

She looks the ram deep in the eyes
her hands smoothe his knobby brow
she wraps her arms around his neck
she waits and waits, then she goes

She looks the lion deep into the eyes
she rubs and brushes his rangy mane
she combs and fans his feathery tail
and waits and waits, then she goes

She looks the wolf deep into the eyes
she scratches his bushy pointed ears
she sees the rising flame in his eyes
she leads the wolf to her chamber

In her magic encircling embrace
he becomes a human, her lover
the one man on earth she needs
to love her.

Music

When she plays her fiddle imitates
all hues and cries of humans
the squealing baby
boys' ballgame shouts
sighs of a young woman
a couple kissing
an old woman who cries

voices from cradle to grave
from sorrow to joy
and back again

Savita Singh

India

Barefoot Thoughts

Come barefoot my thoughts
Come with the lightness of a beautiful night
Come, one by one
Like the blessings of gods
Come as nothing comes
stay with me till the lamp of civilization burns
In pain and in restlessness

Stay as my only witness
While I watch this world asleep

Desire

To call a path mine
A forgotten joy – happiness
To rest in someone's sleep
To wake up in the arms of a sweet dream –
This is my desire tonight

But as it draws to a close
will this path remain kindled?
Joy's hope melted in memory?
Sleep's charm spread in each pore?
Two eyes like swans afloat in my dream?

Translated from the original Hindi by Lucy Rosenstein

I am the House of Stars

Who knows how many stars
fall into my eyes and perish
Their dazzling light,
their scorching heat
extinguished in my eyes
Stars
come to die, like people,
in the vast radiant house I've become

Each and every night
a star descends in me
Its bright light dies
Its great heat disappears
Each and every night

Translated from the original Hindi by Lucy Rosenstein

Woman is Truth

There's sleep all around
Thirst everywhere
In wakefulness too
Even where dreams are awake
Where the ocean sways

One can see afar
The plain concrete lands
A piece of the world somewhat ancient
And there is a woman transgressing thirst

Translated from the original Hindi by Sukrita

Existence

The long afternoon
Like a sordid face
Droops listlessly
On the very edge of the day
Marvelously
Though sad and dispirited are the desires of night

The howling hot wind
Threatens to turn into a storm
The ever-shameless cows are scattered around the field
Chewing and yawning
A pair of sparrows has lost the way to my big room
The noise of their tiny wings
Is mixed with their heart beats
This long afternoon is getting longer than it seems

A perilous silence is this afternoon
I am only a devastating gap in it

A World of Terracotta and Gold

Will you come to see my little world
To recognize the fragile darkness
In which prosper myriad colors and sounds
The utensils stored during my great grandfather's time
Brass, bronze, the glaze less silver,
Self assured gold; but also china, terracotta;
The moth eaten woolens
And the prosperity of the white termites
Settled with their colonies on the books
Long after history has stumbled upon us

Will you come and walk with me
On the narrow path
Which terminates in an alley
Drawn by an artist, patronized by some great uncle
And enter into that dimly lit corner
Where lies stored equipment of power:
Whips, sticks, rifles and plough
But do see closely
There are also odd pieces of instruments of music;
Look how sadly lies a pair of tabla !
And a tattered divan spurned around, drowsing
Still holding hands with the golden chairs

Will you come and see
That a strange person still handcrafts a replica
Of my little world of wonderment
And many darker rooms are being filled with
So much gold and terracotta

Part of the Picture

Everything was simple
Almost right that evening---
Grandfather was in his room
Catching up with the morning news
Reading soon –to- be closed down 'The Searchlight',
Father had returned home after work,
Brother had gone to play cricket in the city's Central Park,
Younger sister was readying herself to complete her homework,
Neighbors were civil and orderly,
Flowers in the garden bloomed enough
Our Parrot in the brass cage hung unflustered in the corner,
Mangoes seating neatly one upon the other on the table,
Radio playing softly Bade Ghulam Ali Khan,
Tears rolling down mother's cheeks,
Her chest shaking in between once in a while

All this was a tranquil picture of life,
In this part of the world, in this time
And I was a part of it, witnessing,
Beholding it, in its melancholic serenity, beguiled.

Our Precious Chatter

We talked about the city
And its birds
We talked about Meera and her eccentric friend,
The summer we spent sleeping at Krishna's terrace
The faces we sketched of the dubious dreamers
Who would cut their throats for love and fidelity
We talked for hours about Shakuntala's loveless life
And also the cruelty of time and fortune in general
We gathered it was difficult to be one with anything
And to have something enduring as one's companion

We knew---
Each moment of this conversation
Had a potential of turning into a chatter
Leaving us to think about talking itself

After all this though,
We left to catch the train knowing
We had come to know the world a bit better

Who's Woman Am I

Whose woman am I
Who is my lord
Whose legs do I massage
Who gives me food to eat
Whose beatings do I take...
Such were her questions
The one who sat on the seat opposite mine in the train
Traveling along with me

Her age around seventy or seventy-five
Her eyes sunk
The flesh hanging loose
On her face plateaus of sorrow
Trenches of abuses

After a lot of thought I said to her
"I am no-one's woman
I am my own woman
I eat my own food
I eat when I feel like
I do not take beatings from anyone
And no one is my lord"

Her eyes filled with strange silence
Oh! How will this woman survive her life

She was in a dilemma
Comprehending everything
I wished to fill her eyes with the pride of my aloneness
Then I said laughing "my life is in fact your own life"
My journey your own
But something happened that you don't know about-
We all know now
That no-one belongs to anyone
All are their own
Drenched with themselves-shining with the right to be

But the journey is not over yet
Many more trenches of abuses are to be crossed still
One or two more oceans of sorrow
Some more plateaus of torment
When finally that woman arrives
With whom you will be surprised even more
Frightened perhaps
You will cry for her life feeling uncertain again
Once again will you wonder how that woman will survive
But she'll laugh just as me
And say
'See I'm liberated
And this sky
The ocean and its waves
This breeze
And the fragrance of nature within it is all mine
And I am far away from the curses and hopes of my ancestors
Completely my own'

Translated from the original Hindi by Lucy Rosenstein

When Montreal was my City

Passing over Rosemond Street
Just as a whole day passes
Crying, regretting over its worthlessness
Not even the night falls naturally here
Just as the trees have vanished in the forest
Lost are the memories of the bygone days
Even the flowers are perhaps not flowers now
The snow too is not snow
What kind of a museum is this city
Of lost people and transformed things

It was not easy to pass
Even through Elmer Street
To cross over the narrow river of gratification
Carrying thirst;
It wasn't easy to say
That this city is sinking
And then on some cold morning reach someone's house
Asking for sleep

Easy it was only
To watch the continuous falling of the snow
Thinking of love and death

Translated from the original Hindi by Sukrita

Ruth's Dream

Ruth had a dream
She had had many such dreams
She was then with her other lovers
This time she was by herself on the bed
And this was a different town
This time the snow had started to fall right from midnight
And outside her home
Early this morning separated the two lovers
After a quarrel

Ruth's dream was not a trivial one
She had seen a philosopher saint
Sitting under a dense tree
Explaining the meaning of being
Language, is the whole universe, he said
And within it only solitude and love are possible

Ruth was doubtful
After all she had forever been within language
But she never got love in return for love
And her solitude was filled with
Torments of father and the timidity of mother
Somehow into it had wandered a few lovers
Who left merely their beds behind

Ruth wishes to see
This dream over and over again
If only to get to know
How to acquire, in language, the warmth of sparkling solitude
How to survive in this city of snow

Translated from the original Hindi by Sukrita

On the Map of My country

So many wounds on the body
Many more on the mind
Even more on the map of the country
A heap of burnt corpses on one side
On the other hangs an unborn baby killed in the womb
slit open

On one side eyes still as stone marble-like
Those who saw sisters daughters and beloveds being raped
Their pinched breasts wounded necks broken arms
Tired devastated countless bodies groaning collapsing
And within such a reality all those surviving women youth
Children aged
Agitated fear stricken in camps of torment.

Translated from the original Hindi by Sukrita

Mushtak Miya's Flight

Doomed, Mushtak Miya was fleeing
He used to run a cafe,
feed thousands of people with
meat, bread, vegetables, lentils, salad
Everyone came and sat on his bench,
drunk water, allayed fatigue and hunger

How could he know that today
his friends' addresses would change
everyone's heart turn into stone?

That he'd have to leave all and flee
with no shelter to stop and rest
Passed sixty, he was too old to run,
his heart sick
He had no choice
but to fall.

Mushtak Miya fell
and thought, let those thirsty for my blood
come and cut my body in half
here on the street
But the rioters wanted more
It was no longer enough
to halve the blood-smeared body

It had to be burned to ashes
Humanity's last trace
had to become cinders

Mushtak Miya turned to ashes
Humanity too
The sword that slew him
still dancing on the street
summoning fire

Translated from the original Hindi by Lucy Rosenstein

End

In a dark village in Karnataka
a peasant family is preparing
to put an end to life's game

A mat spread on the ground
Poison mixed in a cup

The mother looks at her children
sitting on one side
Sees her world one last time
Ties her sari anew, straightens its edge
Sitting across, the peasant – a stilled storm

They look at each other empty-eyed
Then a wail erupts from his throat
and is buried there instantly
Emptiness stares at them
They see it too
There is no fear

Then peace all around
Only the bodies writhe for a while

Translated from the original Hindi by Lucy Rosenstein

Lonely Drama of the Night

This ruinous night preys upon my dreams
Hunting me like a buffalo in some wild field
Desecrating precious objects of my longings
Rebukes my existence

This night:
Beautiful and contemptuous as death
Has entered the last hours of its betrayals

Sukrita

India

Speech

Do you feel
The warp and weft
of dialogue
Getting denser, quieter
on its own
with time moving on

Always beginning
Never ending

Haikus

Terror-struck bees
Buzzing in hornets

Yellow sun
shooting out of
black clouds
....

Buddha in grey stone
Melting in
White peace
....

Through stillness of my walk
The forest dancing in fog
The earth in circles
....

A scream shooting through
The eye of the needle

the baby is born

Just Before Birth

A canvas
empty of colour
a body
kissed by death

A long silent wait
of the foetus
floating in
backwaters of
existence

undefined

before the cry
of anguish

I remain in half light,
Listen to hidden songs

Strain to hear the ebb and flow
Of tides and seas

In the coming darkness
I read you
As the blind read braille.

Tsunami

Footprints of lovers
in intimate dialogue,

Footprints, those of
old infirm fishermen,
dragging in sand

Frolicking footprints
of children

All caressed into oblivion
Each day by the waves

Today...
They've carried away
the footprints, as also
the feet and
bodies over them

How to begin

This way
That way

It has to
Surface on this paper

From the wilderness
Of the forest and its stinging nettles,
Knotted bushes and twigs
It has to emerge
On this vacancy

From the black holes
Of the universes, seen and unseen,
Through meteor storms and
Somersaulting planets
The hand has to appear with
The finger pointing

This way
That way

High and Low

Once again
That language
of silence
of dumbness

Bridges weighed
Under...
....
Between the moon
And the sun
Like the earth
I am yet again
between

rising and setting
....
Big wholesome moon
This month at dawn
looking the sun
In the eye
Defiant

Pilgrim's Progress

Buried in the debris
near the blind well
in the jungle
are a thousand tales
nibbled by scurrying rats
and infected by amnesia

Bits of tales peep out
as if sticking their tongues
through fine slits
in the wrinkled surface
of the heap
hardening over time,
with more and more
thorny creepers and shrubs
gripping the forest
in a net
from which slip out

dead voices severed
from their bodies,

Compressed sighs
rising occasionally
as white smoke

and bouncing as cold echoes
against the walls of the deep black pit

spewing the romance,
hidden snugly,
of times immemorial
in the tunnel built,
as they say, from the
bottom of the well
to his majesty's fort
at Tughlagabad

The flash of light,
an end of the long night,

slides down the spiral steps
to kiss the mouth
of the passage
to the regal splendour
at the other end,
yielding fresh bodies
for the voices
and softening the earth
to impregnate her with a million
more legends of love...

The Mad Woman on the Avenue of Stars

Hanging stars
Suspended in dusk
Stars below
under the feet,

Stars over the head,

Stars wandering away
From lovers' eyes,
Slipping out of children's dreams

Ocean waves
Splashing ripples of colour
Over innocent wonder pulled out
of nursery rhymes

Chinese wrinkles
Giggling and breaking into
shimmering creaks
And vales twinkling

The old woman tearing her hair
squealing in Cantonese glee

clearing cobwebs of silence
that mask multitudes

amidst the din of stars.

New Grammar

This time
He told me a different tale
The tale of...
as if,
of
although,

"As if you are the only one"
"Although you are the only one"

Language of conditions,
of conjunctions

My Lost Diary

Born through the marriage of
Darkness and silence
In the guarded privacy
Of each night
Six bumpy years lay squeezed;

Marked
Not as
Monday, Tuesday or Wednesday
Nor as dates
first, second or third

But with scars and glints

Each alphabet soaked heavy
With phantoms and angels

As I wrote in the diary
Fingers twitched
through the dreams of the
Baby by the side,

Words descending
from the right
and then left
upright, with heads high

Here and there

Parading emblems of
Virtue and vice

Uncurling emotions
Grouses simmering

Hai Raam
At war with the whole world
And with self

Stuck in the sticky cobwebs here

There, lost in crevices
narrow passages

Cracking bird eggs
In their nests

Words talking back
Meanings crawling out

Salt on
Old wounds;

All this
Never in broad daylight
When page by page
Piece by piece

The child ripped the diary

Hours and minutes
Tumbling in glee

Specs of time
Flying out of the window
Like pigeons in freedom.

Parting Again

Sadness sits like
a snake in my belly
turning and twisting
Giving me hysterics
It sits
Hissing subtle threats
of yet another severance,

Emitting warnings
through my glassy, half-closed eyes
Forcing them open
To stone stillness,
A snow silence,
and a reptile alertness

Sadness travels down my spine
reaching my womb…
Your own home
where I held you tight
till you pushed your way
into a world of
Self , identity and
sadness.

Dream Catcher

I must reach the forest in time
Before the break of dawn each day
to pick some dreams
scattered in misty darkness

I must reach
Before the sun crackles
through the leaves of the trees on which
dreams pile up, perching on the branches
through the night

Dreams half-dreamt, fully dreamt-
And those yet to be dreamt-
Like babies, born and unborn,
Crying out for attention,
Making weird faces in sleep

I pick what gets my fancy
Bits from my wrinkled past
The shadowy fragments of future
Mixing in twilight
Droplets of dew
Ready to vanish with sunrise

Each day I come home with a bagful
Of dreams
That drip through the day
For me and all

Each night
I wait for the new dawn.

Of New Lives

What is that,
Yonder, out there?
Not a shadow, not indeed,
But definite contours of
A body reflecting an already tough mind
A stubborn shadow of her own
A fledgling come into a lingering adolescence
With threatening wings
large and awkward

A warring life
Marching in defiance
Deadening the mother, her adventures,
Leaving her cold and alone
A corpse
Inside the tomb
Strangled by fear and caution

Its the daughter giving
Birth to a new mother,
A mother-fledgling fluttering for
Fresh skies and new grounds
For yet another journey.

About the Poets

Zohra Saed was born in Jalalabad (Afghanistan) and came to New York with her family as a child. She received her MFA at Brooklyn College. Her poetry and essays have been published in numerous anthologies and journals. Some of her poems are published in: *This Day: Diaries of American Women,* Ed. Joni B. Cole, Rebecca Joffrey, and B.K. Rakhra (2002); *Chosen Shore: Stories of Immigrants* (Life History),Ed. Ellen Alexander Conley (U. California Press: 2004); *Shattering the Stereotypes: Muslim Women Speak Out,* Ed. Fawzia Afzal Khan (Olive Branch Press: 2005); *Cut Loose,* Ed. Nan Bauer-Maglin (Rutgers U. Press: 2006); *Voices of Resistance: Muslim Women on War, Faith and Sexuality*, Ed. Sarah Hussein (Seal Press: 2006) and most recently in *Cheers to Muses: Contemporary Works by Asian American Women,* Ed. Asian American Women Artists' Association (AAWAA: 2007); *Gallerie International Journal: Afghanistan,* Ed. Bina Sarkar (India: 2009); and in *Speaking for Herself: Asian Women's Writings* (Penguin India Books: 2009). She has performed as part of the cast of the legendary theater director Ping Chong's *Undesirable Elements* in 2000 and in 2007, where the ensemble caste performed at the first National Asian American Theater Festival. Zohra is co-editor, along with Sahar Muradi, of *One Story, Thirty Stories: An Anthology of Contemporary Afghan*

American Literature (University of Arkansas Press, 2010), the first comprehensive collection of emerging Afghan American writers.

Julie Boden is an English poet born in 1960. She is a Birmingham Poet Laureate who, since 2005, has been Poet in Residence at Symphony Hall, Birmingham. As part of this residency she is currently working on the *Piano Room* project with the composer and pianist Steve Tromans. In 2005 she was awarded an Hawthornden Fellowship and this year she has also been awarded a writer's stipend from Can Serrat, Spain. In 2002 she founded the Oasis Café Theatre at the Orange studio in Birmingham, in 2004 she co-founded Poetry Central and from 2004-2009 she was an artistic advisor and a director of the Warwick Words Festival. She has written three collections and two chapbooks: *Beyond the Bullring*, *Cut on the Bias*, *Through the Eye of a Crow*, *Wasted Lives* and *Bluebeard's Wife*. A selection of her poems, *Aheenthi*, is available in Gujarati. In 2007 she co-edited the anthology of women's writing, *Bluebeard's Wives*. Her work is also included in mixed arts installations, exhibitions, libretti and in verse drama scripts for concert, theatre and radio performances. Along with writing poetry, she creates new work with composers, musicians, visual artists, sculptors, storytellers and companies of actors. More information is available at: www.julieboden.co.uk

Clara Janés (Barcelona 1940) has written more than thirty poetry books which include *La indetenible quietud* ("The Unceasing Stillness", 1998) with engravings by Eduardo Chillida, *Arcángel de sombra* ("Archangel of Shadow", City of Melilla Prize 1998), *Los secretos del*

bosque (*The Forest's Secrets*, Jaime Gil de Biedma Prize 2002) *Fractales* (2005), *Río hacia la nada* ("River to nothingness", Torrevieja Prize, 2009, ed. 2010). Her visual poems and images have been exhibited in Spain, Italy and Mexico. Her poems have been translated into more than twenty languages. She has written several books of essays that include *María Zambrano desde la sombra llameante* ("María Zambrano from the blazing shadow", 2010), and with the greatest Spanish contemporary poet, Antonio Gamoneda, a book of conversations: *La realidad y la poesía* (Reality and Poetry, 2010). She has also published many studies about poetry, particularly on the Spanish and Iranian mystical. Clara Janés is a well known translator of poetry too, especially from Tcheque, French, English, Portuguese, Italian, German. She was honoured with the National Literary Prize Teresa de Avila in 2007, the National Translation Prize in 1997, in 1992 with the Turkish Tutav Fundation Prize, and in 2000, with the First Category Medal of Merit from the Tcheque Republic.

Kishwar Naheed, a major Urdu poet in Pakistan, is a postgraduate in Economics, who has a long experience of management of office & financial matters, in addition to her equally long experience of writing for the media and films. She has handled a number of important projects for the welfare of women including that of promotion of small entrepreneurship, income-generating projects, empowerment of urban poor, as also that of women's craft cooperatives.

Kishwar Naheed has published 11 collections of her poetry in Pakistan itself while several collections of hers have been published elsewhere, in India, Europe and the USA. She has also translated many world poets and edited many anthologies of women's poetry. A well-travelled person, she has delivered lectures and given readings all over the world. For her immense contribution to women's literature, Kishwar was honoured with the Sitara-e-Imtiaz, the prestigious award by the Government of Pakistan. In fact she has been awarded several other international awards including the Mandela and the UNESCO Awards.

Ute Margaret Saine was born in Nuremberg, Germany. After a doctorate in French and Spanish literature from Yale University she moved to California to teach languages, literatures and cultures especially of the Hispanic world. She has lectured in various Latin American countries. Saine writes poetry in five languages and also translates from and into the five. She is a literary editor too and has published many scholarly articles on literature. She is currently working on prose fiction based on her travels. Formerly, president of the PEN Club Orange County, she wrote many letters on behalf of incarcerated writers worldwide. Her books of poetry are *Bodyscapes, Words of Art*, and three chapbooks that include haiku in five languages: *random light—spots of time, Body & Parts--Corpo & Parti* and *haiku di venerdì*. *Awkward Child* is a memoir of her postwar childhood (in German, to be published in Germany), and *The Five Senses* is a manuscript of poetry (tbp). Her poems have been published in the United States and abroad, including on the Internet.

Savita Singh received her post-graduation degree from the University of Delhi and went to McGill University, Montreal, for higher studies. She wrote her Ph.D thesis on "Discourse of Modernity in India: A Hermeneutical

Study." She has been publishing poetry in both Hindi and English. Her first collection *Apne Jaisa Jeevan* (A Life Like its Own) won her a lot of acclaim and she received Delhi's Hindi Academy Award in 2002. Her second collection entitled *Neend Thi Aur Raat Thi* (There was Sleep and There was Night) appeared in 2005. For this she received the prestigious Indo-French "Raza Award". Established as a strong woman poet in Hindi, she published a bilingual collection of poems (Hindi and English) with Sukrita Paul Kumar, *Rowing Together* (2008) and also her bilingual collection (French and Hindi) *je suis la maison des` etoiles* appeared in 2008. Her poems are translated in many Indian and foreign languages such as Spanish, German, French, English and Dutch.

Savita Singh has also published short stories of which "Alas! Lebanon" received special critical notice. Currently she is working on her collection of short stories and three manuscripts of meditative and explorative prose which are at different stages of completion. Her special areas of concern are, feminist politics, epistemology, Indian modernity and women. Currently, Savita Singh is Professor and Director, School of Gender and Development Studies, Indira Gandhi National Open University (IGNOU), Delhi.

Sukrita Paul Kumar, poet and critic, was born and brought up in Kenya. Currently she lives in Delhi and teaches literature. An Honorary Fellow of International Writing Programme, University of Iowa (USA), Cambridge Seminars and a former Fellow of the Indian Institute of Advanced Study, Shimla, she was also an invited poet in residence at Hong Kong Baptist University. A recipient of many international fellowships and residencies, she has published several collections of poems in English including *Poems Come Home, Rowing Together, Without Margins* and *Folds of Silence*. She was the Guest Editor of *Crossing Over*, a special issue of "Manoa"(University of Hawaii, USA).

Sukrita's major critical works include *Narrating Partition, Conversations on Modernism, The New Story* and *Man, Woman and Androgyny*. Some of her edited/ co-edited books include *Ismat, Her Life, Her Times; Interpreting Homes in South Asian Literature*. As Director of a UNESCO project on "The Culture of Peace", she edited *Mapping Memories*, a volume of Urdu short stories from India and Pakistan. She has two books of translations, *Stories of Joginder Paul* and the novel *Sleepwalkers*. She is the chief editor of the book on *Cultural Diversity in India* (Macmillan India). Her latest co-edited book is *Speaking for Herself*, an anthology of Asian women's writings (Penguin). A solo exhibition of her paintings was held at AIFACS, Delhi. A number of Sukrita's poems have emerged from her experience of working with homeless people, Tsunami victims and street children.

❑❑❑